NICODEMUS LEARNS THE WAY

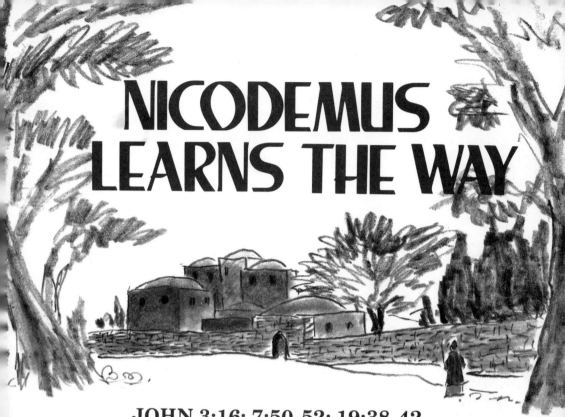

JOHN 3:16; 7:50-52; 19:38-42

FOR CHILDREN

Written by Yvonne Patterson
Illustrated by Betty Wind

ARCH Books

Copyright © 1982 CONCORDIA PUBLISHING HOUSE
ST. LOUIS, MISSOURI
MANUFACTURED IN THE UNITED STATES OF AMERICA
ALL RIGHTS RESERVED
ISBN 0-570-06152-0

D1570806

There was a man of the Pharisees—
a leader of the Jews.
His name was Nicodemus,
and he'd heard the latest news:

news about Jesus—a Prophet,
a Teacher, a King.
He knew He even cured the sick
and healed the lame and everything.

Few men before had done such things.
Could He be the Promised One?
"I must find out," thought Nicodemus.
So . . . after the setting of the sun,
Nicodemus went secretly to the place
where Jesus was staying.

He was afraid that Jesus might be sleeping,
or maybe He'd be too busy praying.
Whatever it was He was doing,
Jesus was glad to welcome him in.

"I've heard so much about You—
of all the things You've done.
Do You know the way to heaven?
Could it be You are God's Son?"

Then Jesus kindly replied to the man,
"Nicodemus, there's only one way.
You must be born again."

"Born again? Born again, You say?
How can a man be born again?
I just don't understand?"

Jesus answered, "Believe in Me.
You don't have to be born as a baby again.
You simply *believe* in the Son of God,
and you're part of *His* family then!
For God loved the world so very much
that He sent His only Son to die,
and anyone believing this
will someday live with Him on high."

From that night on, Jesus must have been
in Nicodemus' every thought.
He heard how Jesus continued to preach
and of the great truths He taught.

But the other leaders were all upset
to hear so many believed.
"They'll follow *Him*, instead of us!"
they cried, for they were sorely grieved.

"Bring that Jesus here to us!"
the priests commanded their men.
"We'll kill that traitor.
Then He'll never preach those lies again!"

But when the priests' officers returned,
they were all alone.
"We couldn't bring Him in," they said.
"He's like no one we've ever known!"

Then Nicodemus spoke up,
"We must do according to our law.
He can't be killed without a trial.
And His offenses none of us saw."

The priests shouted at Nicodemus,
"Oh, do you believe in Him then?"
Nicodemus said no more.

He had a nice home and a very good job.
Nicodemus was an important man.
He said to himself, "I tried anyway.
I've got too much to lose;
I've done all I can."

But soon the day arrived
when Nicodemus heard the awful news.
"They're taking Jesus to the cross!"
the cry spread throughout the land.
Then Nicodemus remembered Jesus telling him
that this is exactly what God had planned.

Nicodemus went to see his friend Joseph
when he heard that Jesus had died.
The two men made plans together,
and the two of them also cried.

Joseph owned a new tomb,
and they knew just what to do.
They were going to bury their Savior,
and they didn't care who knew.

Joseph of Arimathaea was a counselor
and a very rich man.
He begged Pilate, "May I take Jesus' body?"
And Pilate said, "You can."

The two men took Jesus down from the cross,
and they carried Him away.
For all of Jesus' followers
this was the saddest day.

Nicodemus brought some costly spices,
and they wrapped Him in cloths of white.
Then they laid Him in the garden tomb,
and that was the first night.

Jesus came back to life
the morning of the third day.
And, as Nicodemus learned long ago,
JESUS IS THE WAY.

DEAR PARENTS:

The Pharisees were proud men. They despised Jesus and refused to believe that He was the Son of God. Nicodemus, however, wanted to know more about Jesus' teachings; he believed this "teacher come from God" had a wonderful message and should be heard.

Christ used Nicodemus' nighttime visit to teach him (and us) the most important truth anyone can learn—how to become a member of God's family: "Unless one is born of water and the Spirit, he cannot enter the kingdom of God" (John 3:5 RSV).

Not by strictly keeping the Law, not by doing good deeds, not by earning God's favor do we become part of God's kingdom; it is through a total change of heart that we are received into His family. It is a change so complete that it is like being born a second time.

Baptism is the means by which the Holy Spirit works this change, this new birth in us. Through Baptism we become "partakers of the promise of Christ Jesus" (Ephesians 3:6), the promise Jesus so clearly expressed to Nicodemus: "God so loved the world that He gave His only Son, that whoever believes in Him should not perish but have eternal life" (John 3:16).

At the death of Christ on Calvary, Nicodemus was a witness to the depth of God's love. Although no more is written of him after the burial of Jesus, it is likely that Nicodemus was also a witness to the glory of the Resurrection. If he himself did not see the risen Christ, he would have at least heard the joyful news through the apostles.

Tell your child of the love that God has for his family and for all people. He loves us so much that He sent His own Son to suffer our punishment and to redeem us "from all sins, from death, and from the power of the devil."

THE EDITOR